A Sketch of the Life and Labors of

GEORGE WHITEFIELD

By J. C. Ryle

This is Volume #8 in the Works of J. C. Ryle series.

This annotated edition of *A Sketch of the Life and Labors of George Whitefield:*

* Has been enriched by additional historical content providing context and setting to the various chapters of the book

* Includes, among other items, a glossary of people and terms mentioned in the introduction, as well as comments about George Whitefield by his friend Ben Franklin

Annotated content is presented in italics throughout the book.

ISBN #978-1611047059

Table of Contents

Introduction

There are some men in the pages of history whose greatness no person of common sense thinks of disputing. They tower above the herd of mankind, like the pyramids, the Parthenon, and the Colosseum, among buildings. Such men were Luther and Augustine, Gustavus Adolphus and George Washington, Columbus and Sir Isaac Newton. He who questions their greatness must be content to be thought very ignorant, very prejudiced, or very eccentric. Public opinion has come to a conclusion about them—they were great men.

But there are also great men whose reputation lies buried under a heap of contemporary ill-will and misrepresentation. The world does not appreciate them, because the world does not know their real worth. Their characters have come down to us through poisoned channels. Their portraits have been drawn by the ill-natured hand of enemies. Their faults have been exaggerated. Their excellences have been maliciously kept back and suppressed. Like the famous sculptures of Nineveh, they need the hand of some literary Layard to clear away the rubbish that has accumulated round their names and show them to the world in their fair proportions. Such men were Vigilantius and Wickliffe. Such men were Oliver Cromwell and many of the Puritans. And such a man was George Whitefield.

There are few men whose characters have suffered so much from ignorance and misrepresentation of the truth as Whitefield's.

That he was a famous Methodist, an ally of John Wesley, in the last century; that he was much run after by ignorant people, for his preaching; that many thought him an enthusiast and fanatic; all this is about as much as most Englishmen know.

But that he was one of the principal champions of Evangelical religion in the eighteenth century in our own country; that he was one of the most powerful and effective preachers that ever lived; that he was a man of extraordinary singleness of eye, and devotedness to the interests of true religion; that he was a regularly ordained clergyman of the Church of England, and would always have worked in the church, if the church had not, most unwisely, shut him out; all these are things of which few people seem aware. And yet, after calm examination of his life and writings, I am satisfied this is the true account that ought to be given of George Whitefield.

My chief desire is to assist in forming a just estimate of Whitefield's worth. I wish to lend a helping hand towards raising his name from the undeservedly low place which is commonly assigned to it. I wish to place him before your eyes as a noble specimen of what the grace of God can enable one man to do. I want you to treasure up his name in your memories, as one of the brightest in that company of departed saints who were, in their day, patterns of good works, and of whom the world was not worthy.

I propose, therefore, without further preface, to give you a hasty sketch of Whitefield's times, Whitefield's life, Whitefield's religion, Whitefield's preaching, and Whitefield's actual work on earth.

J. C. Ryle

* * * * *

Glossary of People and Terms

Parthenon: *An ancient temple that dominates the hill of the Acropolis at Athens, the Parthenon was built in the mid-5th century BCE when the Athenian Empire was at the peak of its power. Dedicated to the Greek goddess Athena, the temple is generally considered to be the culmination of the development of the Doric order, the simplest of the three Classical Greek architectural orders.*

Colliseum: *The Colosseum an oval amphitheatre in the centre of the city of Rome, Italy. Built of travertine, tuff, and brick-faced concrete, it is the largest amphitheatre ever built. The Colosseum is situated just east of the Roman Forum.*

Martin Luther: *Martin Luther (1483 - 1546) was a German monk who began the Protestant Reformation in the 16th century, becoming one of the most influential and controversial figures in Christian history. Luther called into question some of the basic tenets of Roman Catholicism, and his followers, known as Protestants, soon split from the Roman Catholic Church. A prominent theologian, Luther's desire for people to feel closer to God led him to translate the Bible into the language of the people, radically changing the relationship between church leadership and church members.*

Augustine: *Augustine of Hippo was a Roman African, early Christian theologian and philosopher from Numidia whose writings influenced the development of Western Christianity and philosophy.*

Gustavus Adolphus: *Gustav II Adolf (1594 – 1632), widely known as Gustavus Adolphus, was the Swedish king credited with the founding of his country as a great power. He led Sweden to military supremacy during the Thirty Years' War, helping to determine the political as well as the religious balance of power in Europe.*

George Washington: *One of the Founding Fathers of the United States, George Washington (1732 – 1799) served as the nation's first President and is today often recognized as the "Father of His Country.". During the American Revolutionary War he commanded Patriot forces to victory against the British and their allies. He also presided over the Constitutional Convention of 1787, which established the new federal government.*

Columbus: *Christopher Columbus (1451 – 1506) was an Italian explorer, navigator, and colonist who completed four voyages across the Atlantic Ocean under the auspices of the Catholic Monarchs of Spain. He led the first European expeditions to the Caribbean, Central America, and South America, initiating the permanent European colonization of the Americas.*

Sir Isaac Newton: *Sir Isaac Newton (1642 – 1726) was an English mathematician, astronomer, theologian, author and physicist who is widely recognised as one of the most influential scientists of all time and a key figure in the scientific revolution. His book Philosophiæ Naturalis Principia Mathematica ("Mathematical Principles of Natural Philosophy"), first published in 1687, laid the foundations of classical mechanics. Newton also made significant contributions to the fields of optics and calculus.*

Sculptures of Ninevah: *Nineveh was an ancient Assyrian city located on the outskirts of Mosul in modern-day northern Iraq. It was the largest city in the world for some fifty years until the year 612 BC when it was sacked after a bitter period of civil war in Assyria. The ruins of Ninevah lie across the river from the modern-day major city of Mosul. Large amounts of Assyrian sculpture and other artifacts have been excavated and are now located in museums around the world.*

Layard: *Sir Austen Henry Layard (1817 – 1894) was an English traveller, archaeologist, cuneiformist, art historian, draughtsman, collector, politician and diplomat. He is best known as the excavator of Nimrud and of Nineveh, where he uncovered a large proportion of the Assyrian palace reliefs known, and in 1851 the library of Ashurbanipal.*

Vigilantius: *Vigilantius (370 - 406) is credited with being the leader of the Waldensees, a group of people who formed a resistance to the moral corruption and physically damaging* *practices advocated by the system of monasticism that blossomed under the papacy.. Himself a peasant, Vigilantius on the role of defending the church against the growing pagan practices of the time.*

Wyckliffe: *John Wycliffe (1330 - 1384) was an English scholastic philosopher, theologian, Biblical translator, reformer, English priest, and a seminary professor at the University of Oxford. He was an influential dissident within the Roman Catholic priesthood during the 14th century and is considered an important predecessor to Protestantism.*

Oliver Cromwell: *Oliver Cromwell (1599 - 1658) was an English military and political leader. Oliver Cromwell played a leading role in bringing Charles I to trial and execution, and was a key figure during the civil war of that era.*

Puritans: *The Puritans were English Reformed Protestants in the 16th and 17th centuries who sought to "purify" the Church of England from its Catholic practices, maintaining that the Church of England was only partially reformed. Puritanism played a significant role in English history, especially during The Protectorate.*

John Wesley: *John Wesley (1703 - 1791) was an English cleric and theologian who, with his brother Charles and fellow cleric George Whitefield, founded Methodism. Doctrinally, Wesley is best known for his emphasis on free grace, sanctification, and perfection.*

Chapter 1: The Times of George Whitefield

The story of Whitefield's times is one that should often be told. Without it, nobody is qualified to form an opinion either as to the man or his acts. Conduct that in one kind of times may seem rash, extravagant, and indiscreet, in another may be wise, prudent, and even absolutely necessary. In forming your opinion of the comparative merits of Christian men, never forget the old rule: "Distinguish between times." Place yourself in each man's position. Do not judge what was a right course of action in other times, by what seems a right course of action in your own.

Now, the times when Whitefield lived were, unquestionably, the worst times that have ever been known in this country since the Protestant Reformation. There never was a greater mistake than to talk of "the good old times." The times of the eighteenth century, at any rate, were "bad old times," unmistakably. Whitefield was born in 1714. He died in 1770. It is not saying too much to assert, that this was precisely the darkest age that England has passed through in the last three hundred years. Anything more deplorable than the condition of the country, as to religion, morality, and high principle, from 1700 to about the era of the French Revolution, it is very difficult to conceive.

The state of religion in the established ehurch can only be compared to that of a frozen or palsied carcass. There were the time-honored formularies which the wisdom of the Reformers had provided. There were the services and lessons from Scripture, just in the same order as we have them now. But, as to preaching the gospel in the established church, there was almost none. The distinguishing doctrines of Christianity—the atonement, the work and office of Christ and the Spirit—were comparatively lost sight of. The vast majority of sermons were miserable moral essays, utterly devoid of any thing calculated to awaken, convert, save, or sanctify souls. The curse of black Bartholomew-day seemed to rest upon our Church. For at least a century after casting out two thousand of the best ministers in England, our establishment never prospered.

There were some learned and conscientious bishops at this era, beyond question. Such men were Secker, and Gibson, and Lowth, and Warburton, and Butler, and Horne. But even the best of them sadly misunderstood the requirements of the day they lived in. They spent their strength in writing apologies for Christianity and contending against infidels. They could not see that, without the direct preaching of the essential doctrines of Christ's gospel, their labors were all in vain. And as to the majority of the bishops, they were potent for negative evil, but impotent for positive good; giants at stopping what they thought disorder, but infants at devising anything to promote real order; mighty to repress overzealous attempts at evangelization, but weak to put in action any remedy for the evils of the age; eagle-eyed at detecting any unhappy wight who trod on the toes of a rubric or canon, but blind as bats to the flood of indolence and false doctrine with which their dioceses were everywhere deluged.

That there were many well-read, respectable and honorable men among the parochial clergy at this period, it would be wrong to deny. But few, it is to be feared, out of the whole number, preached Christ crucified in simplicity and sincerity. Many whose lives were decent and moral were notoriously Arians, if not Socinians. Many were totally engrossed in secular pursuits; they neither did good themselves, nor liked anyone else to do it for them. They hunted; they shot; they drank; they swore; they fiddled; they farmed; they toasted church and king and thought little or nothing about saving souls. And as for the man who dared to preach the doctrine of the Bible, the Articles, and the Homilies, he was sure to be set down as an enthusiast and fanatic.

The state of religion among the Dissenters was only a few degrees better than the state of the church. The toleration which they enjoyed from William the Third's time was certainly productive of a very bad spiritual effect on them as a body. As soon as they ceased to be persecuted, they appear to have gone to sleep. The Baptist and Independent could still point to Gill, and Guyse, and Doddridge, and Watts, and a few more like-minded men. But the English Presbyterians were fast lapsing into Socinianism. And as to the great majority of nonconformists, it is vain to deny that they were very different men from Baxter, and Flavel, and Gurnall, and Traill. A generation of preachers arose who were very orthodox, but painfully cold; very conscientious, but very wanting in spirituality; very constant in their objections to the established church, but very careless about spreading vital Christianity.

I deeply feel the difficulty of conveying a correct impression of the times when Whitefield lived. I dislike overstatement as much as anyone, but I am thoroughly persuaded it is not easy to make an overstatement on this branch of my subject.

These were the times when the highest personages in the realm lived openly in ways which were flatly contrary to the law of God, and no man rebuked them. No courts, I suppose, can be imagined more diametrically unlike than the courts of George I and George II and the court of Queen Victoria.

These were the times when profligacy and irreligion were reputable and respectable things. Judging from the description we have of men and manners in those days, a gentleman might have been defined as a creature who got drunk, gambled, swore, fought duels, and broke the seventh commandment incessantly. And for all this, no one thought the worse of him.

These were the days when the men whom kings delighted to honor were Bolingbroke, Chesterfield, Walpole, and Newcastle. To be an infidel or a skeptic, to obtain power by intrigue, and to retain power by the grossest and most notorious bribery, were considered no disqualifications at this era. Such was the utter want of religion, morality, and high principle in the land, that men such as these were not only tolerated, but praised.

These were the days when Hume, the historian, put forth his work, became famous, and got a pension. He was notoriously an infidel. These were the days when Sterne and Swift wrote their clever, but most indecent productions. Both were clergymen, and high in the church; but the public saw no harm. These were the days when Fielding and Smollet were the popular authors, and the literary taste of high and low was suited by Roderick Random, Peregrine Pickle, Joseph Andrews, and Tom Jones.

These were the days when Knox says, in his history of Christian Philosophy: "Some of the most learned men—the most voluminous writers on theological subjects—were totally ignorant of Christianity. They were ingenious heathen philosophers, assuming the name of Christians, and forcibly paganizing Christianity, for the sake of pleasing the world." These were the days when Archbishop Drummond (1760) could talk of "intricate and senseless questions, about the influence of the Spirit the power of grace, predestination, imputed righteousness, justification without works, and other opinions which have from the beginning perplexed and perverted, debased, defiled, and wounded Christianity." These were the days when Bishop Warburton considered the teaching office of the Holy Spirit to be completed in the Holy Scriptures, and that his sanctifying and comforting offices are chiefly confined to charity. Such were the leading ministers. What must the mass of teachers have been! Such were the priests of Whitefield's time. What must have been the people!

These were the days when there was an utter dearth of sound theological writing. The doctrines of the Reformers were trampled underfoot by men who sat in their chairs. The bread of the church was eaten by men who flatly contradicted her Articles. The appetite of religious people was satisfied with "Tillotson's Sermons," and the "Whole Duty of Man." A pension of two hundred pounds a year was actually given to Blair, of Edinburgh, for writing his most unchristian sermons. Ask any theological bookseller, and he will tell you that, generally speaking, no divinity is so worthless as that of the eighteenth century.

These were the days when there was no Society for promoting the increase of true religion, but the *Christian Knowledge Society*, and the *Society for the Propagation of the Gospel.* And even their work was comparatively trifling. Nothing was done for the Jew. Nothing was done for the heathen. Nothing, almost, was done for the colonies. Nothing was done for the destitute parts of our own country. Nothing was done for education. The church slept. The dissenters slept. The pulpit slept. The religious press slept. The gates were left wide open. The walls were left unguarded. Infidelity stalked in. The Devil sowed tares broadcast and walked to and fro. The gentry gloried in their shame, and no man pointed out their wickedness. The people sinned with a high hand, and no man taught them better. Ignorance, profligacy, irreligion, and superstition, were to be seen everywhere. Such were the times when Whitefield was raised up.

I know that this is a dreadful picture. I marvel God did not sweep away the church altogether. But I believe that the picture is not one whit too highly colored. It is painful to expose such a state of things. But, for Whitefield's sake, the truth ought to be known. Justice has not been done to him, because the condition of the times he lived in is not considered. The times he lived in were extraordinary times and required extraordinary means to be used. And whatever quiet men, sitting by their fireside in our day, may say to the contrary, I am satisfied that Whitefield was just the man for his times.

* * * * *

Historical Notes

Today, many historians view the England of the 1700s as a moral and spiritual cesspool. Thomas Carlyle, the great Scottish philosopher of that era, described the country's condition as "Stomach well alive, soul extinct." Deism was rampant, and a bland, philosophical morality was standard fare in the churches. Sir William Blackstone, who visited the church of every major clergyman in London, claimed that he didn't "hear a single discourse which had more Christianity in it than the writings of Cicero." In most sermons he heard, it would have been impossible to tell just from listening whether the preacher was a follower of Confucius, Mohammed, or Christ.

Drunkenness was rampant, and gambling was so extensive in the country that a historian described England as "one vast casino." 97% of the infant poor in the workhouses died as children. Bear baiting and cock fighting were accepted sports, and tickets were sold to public executions as to a theater. The slave trade brought material gain to many while further degrading their souls. Bishop Berkeley wrote that morality and religion in Britain had collapsed "to a degree that was never known in any Christian country."

That was the state of things in England when George Whitefield, who was converted in 1737, arrived on the scene in London as Bristol as "one of God's runabouts," his nickname for himself as a traveling minister.

Chapter 2: The Life of George Whitefield

The story of Whitefield's life, which forms the next part of our subject, is one that is soon told. The facts and incidents of that life are few and simple, and I shall not dwell upon them at any length.

Whitefield was born in 1714. Like many other great men, he was of very humble origin. His father and mother kept the Bell Inn, in the city of Gloucester. Whether there is such an inn now, I do not know. But, judging from Whitefield's account of his circumstances, it must formerly have been a very small concern.

Whitefield's early life seems to have been anything but religious, though he had occasional fits of devout feeling. He speaks of himself as having been addicted to lying, filthy talking, and foolish jesting. He confesses that he was a Sabbath-breaker, a theater-goer, a card-player, and a romance-reader. All this went on till he was twelve or fifteen years old.

At the age of twelve he was placed at a grammar school in Gloucester. Little is known of his progress there, excepting the curious fact that even then he was remarkable for his good elocution and memory, and was selected to make speeches before the corporation at their annual visitations.

At the age of fifteen he appears to have become tired of Latin and Greek, and to have given up all hopes of ever becoming more than a tradesman. He ceased to take lessons in anything but writing. He began to assist his mother in the public-house that she kept. "At length," he says, "I put on my blue apron, washed mops, cleaned rooms, and, in one word, became a professed common drawer for nigh a year and a half."

But God, who ordereth all things in heaven and earth, and called David from keeping sheep to be a king, had provided some better thing for Whitefield than the office of a pot-boy. Family disagreements interfered with his prospects at the Bell Inn. An old schoolfellow stirred up again within him the desire of going to the university. And at length, after several providential circumstances had smoothed the way, he was launched, at the age of eighteen, at Oxford, in a position at that time much more humbling than it is now, as a servitor at Pembroke College.

Whitefield's Oxford career seems to have been the turning point in his life. According to his own journal, he had not been without religious convictions for two or three years before he went to Oxford. From the time of his entering Pembroke College, these convictions rapidly ripened into decided Christianity. He became marked for his attendance on all means of grace within his reach. He spent his leisure time in visiting the city prisons and doing good. He formed an acquaintance with the famous John Wesley and his brother Charles, which gave a color to the whole of his subsequent life. At one time he seems to have had a narrow escape from becoming a semi-papist, an ascetic, or a mystic. From this he seems to have been delivered, partly by the advice of wiser and more experienced Christians, and partly by reading such books as Scougal's *Life of God in the Soul of Man,* Law's *Serious Call*, Baxter's *Call to the Unconverted*, and Alleine's *Alarm to Unconverted Sinners*. At length, in 1736, at the early age of twenty-two, he was ordained deacon by Bishop Benson, of Gloucester, and began to run that ministerial race in which he never drew breath till he was laid in the grave.

His first sermon was preached in St. Mary-le-Crypt, Gloucester. It was said to have driven fifteen persons mad. Bishop Benson remarked, that he only hoped the madness might continue. He next accepted temporary duty at the Tower Chapel, London. While engaged there, he preached continually in many of the London churches, and among others, in the parish churches of Islington, Bishopsgate, St. Dunstan's, St. Margaret, Westminster, and Bow, Cheapside. From the very beginning he attained a degree of popularity such as no preacher, probably, before or since, has ever reached. To say that the churches were crowded when he preached, would be saying little. They were literally crammed to suffocation. An eye-witness said, "You might have walked on the people's heads."

From London he removed for a few months to Dummer, a little rural parish in Hampshire, near Basingstoke. From Dummer he sailed for the colony of Georgia, in North America, after visiting Gloucester and Bristol, and preaching in crowded churches in each place. The object of his voyage was to assist the Wesleys in the care of an orphan house which they had established in Georgia for the children of colonists who died there. The management of this orphan house ultimately devolved entirely on Whitefield, and entailed on him a world of responsibility and anxiety all his life long. Though well meant, it seems to have been a design of very questionable wisdom. (This orphan house at Savannah is now in a flourishing condition, and of great usefulness.)

Whitefield returned from Georgia after about two years' absence, partly to obtain priest's orders, which were conferred on him by Bishop Benson, and partly on business connected with the orphan house. And now we reach the era in his life when he was obliged, by circumstances, to take up a line of conduct as a minister which he probably at one time never contemplated, but which was made absolutely necessary by the treatment he received.

It appears that, on arriving in London after his first visit to Georgia, he found the countenances of many of the clergy no longer towards him as they were before. They had taken fright at some expressions in his published letters, and some reports of his conduct in America. They were scandalized at his preaching the doctrine of regeneration in the way that he did, as a thing which many of their parishioners needed. The pulpits of many churches were flatly refused to him. Churchwardens, who had no eyes for heresy and drunkenness, were filled with virtuous indignation about what they called breaches of order. Bishops who could tolerate Arianism and Socinianism, got into a state of excitement about a man who simply preached the gospel and put forth warnings against fanaticism and enthusiasm. In short, Whitefield's field of usefulness within the church was rapidly narrowed on every side.

The step which seems to have decided Whitefield's course of action at this period of his life was his adoption of open-air preaching. He had gone to Islington on a Sunday in April, 1739, to preach for the vicar, his friend, Mr. Stonehouse. In the midst of the prayers, the churchwarden came to him, and demanded his license for preaching in the London diocese. This Whitefield, of course, had not got, any more than any clergyman not regularly officiating in the diocese has at this day. The upshot of the matter was, that being forbidden to preach in the pulpit, he went outside after the service and preached in the churchyard. From that day, he regularly took up the practice of open-air preaching. Wherever there were large open fields around London; wherever there were large bands of idle, church-despising, Sabbath-breaking people gathered together—there went Whitefield and lifted up his voice.

The gospel so proclaimed was listened to, and greedily received by hundreds who had never dreamed of visiting a place of worship. In Moorfields, in Hackney Fields, in Mary-le-bone Fields, in May Fair, in Smithfield, on Kennington Common, on Blackheath, Sunday after Sunday, Whitefield preached to admiring masses. Ten thousand, fifteen thousand, twenty thousand, thirty thousand, were computed sometimes to have heard him at once. The cause of pure religion, beyond doubt, was advanced. Souls were plucked from the hand of Satan as brands from the burning. But it was going much too fast for the church of those days. The clergy, with very few exceptions, would have nothing to do with this strange preacher. In short, the ministrations of Whitefield in the pulpits of the establishment, with an occasional exception, from this time ceased. He loved the church. He gloried in her Articles and Formularies. He used her *Prayer Book* with delight. But the church did not love him, and so lost the use of his services. The plain truth is, the Church of England of that day was not ready for a man like Whitefield. The church was too much asleep to understand him.

From this date to the day of his death, a period of thirty-one years, Whitefield's life was one uniform employment. From Sunday morning to Saturday night—from the 1st of January to the 31st of December—excepting when laid aside by illness, he was almost incessantly preaching. There was hardly a considerable town in England, Scotland,

and Wales, that he did not visit. When churches were opened to him, he gladly preached in churches. When chapels only were offered, he cheerfully preached in chapels. When church and chapel alike were closed, he was ready and willing to preach in the open air. For thirty-four years he labored in this way, always proclaiming the same glorious gospel, and always, as far as a man's eye can judge, with immense effect. In one single Whitsuntide week, after he had been preaching in Moorfields, he received one thousand letters from people under spiritual concern, and admitted to the Lord's table three hundred and fifty persons. In the thirty-four years of his ministry, it is reckoned that he preached publicly eighteen thousand times.

His journeyings were prodigious, when the roads and conveyances of his times are considered. Fourteen times did he visit Scotland. Seven times did he cross the Atlantic, backward and forward. Twice he went over to Ireland. As to England and Wales, he traversed every county in them, from the Isle of Wight to Berwick-on-Tweed, and from the Land's End to the North Foreland.

His regular ministerial work in London, when he was not journeying, was prodigious. His weekly engagements at the Tabernacle in Tottenham-court Road, which was built for him when the pulpits of the established church were closed, were as follows: Every Sunday morning he administered the Lord's Supper to several hundred communicants, at half-past six. After this he read prayers, and preached, both morning and afternoon; preached again in the evening at half-past five; and concluded, by addressing a large society of widows, married people, young men and spinsters, all sitting separately in the area of the tabernacle, with exhortations suitable to their respective stations. On Monday, Tuesday, Wednesday, and Thursday mornings, he preached regularly at six. On Monday, Tuesday, Wednesday, Thursday, and Saturday evenings, he delivered lectures. This you will observe made thirteen sermons a week. And all this time he was carrying on a correspondence with people in almost every part of the world.

That any human frame could so long endure the labor he went through, does indeed seem wonderful. That his life was not shortened by violence, is no less wonderful. Once he was nearly stoned to death by a popish mob in Dublin. Once he was nearly murdered in bed by an angry lieutenant of the navy at Plymouth. Once he narrowly escaped being stabbed by the sword of a rakish young gentleman in Moorfields; but he was immortal till his work was done. He died at last at Newburyport, in North America, from a fit of asthma, at the age of fifty-six. His last sermon was preached only twenty-four hours before his death. It was an open-air discourse two hours long. Like Bishop Jewell, he almost died preaching. He left no children. He was once married, and the marriage does not seem to have contributed much to his happiness. But he left a name far better than that of sons and daughters. Never, I believe, was there a man of whom it could be so truly said, that he spent and was spent for God.

* * * * *

Historical Notes

Though born in humble beginnings, today George Whitefield is known as the Church of England evangelist who, by his popular open air preaching, stimulated the 18th-century Protestant revival throughout Britain and the British American colonies.

In his school and college days Whitefield experienced a strong religious awakening that he called a "new birth." At Oxford he became an intimate of the Methodists John and Charles Wesley, and at their invitation he joined them in their missionary work in the American colony of Georgia in 1738. By this time, Whitefield was already known as an eloquent evangelist.

The remainder of Whitefield's career, from that time forward, was divided between evangelical preaching throughout the American colonies from Georgia to Massachusetts and itinerant preaching in England, Scotland, Wales, and Ireland. Believing that every truly religious person needs to experience a rebirth in Jesus, Whitefield cared little for distinctions of denomination or geography. He played a leading part in the Great Awakening of religious life in the British American colonies and in the early Methodist movement.

Chapter 3: The Religion of George Whitefield

The story of Whitefield's religion is the next part of the subject that I proposed to take up, and unquestionably it is one of no little interest.

What sort of doctrine did this wonderful man preach? an inquirer may reasonably ask. What were the standards of faith to which he adhered under the Bible? What were the peculiar essentials of this religious teaching of his, which was so universally spoken against in his day?

The answer to all these questions is short and simple. Whitefield was a real, genuine son of the Church of England. As such he was brought up in early youth. As such he was educated at Oxford. As such he preached as long as he was allowed to preach within the establishment. As such he preached when he was outside. References to the *Prayer Book,* Articles, and Homilies, abound in all his writings and sermons. His constant reply to his numerous opponents was, that *he* at any rate was consistent with the formularies of his own Church, and that *they* were not. It is not at all too much to say, that when practically cast out of the establishment, Whitefield was an infinitely better churchman than ten thousand of the men who received the tithes of the Church of England, and remained comfortably behind.

Whitefield no doubt was not a churchman of the stamp of Archbishop Laud and his school. He was not the man to put a Romish interpretation on our excellent Formularies, and to place church and sacraments before Christ. He was not a churchman of the stamp of Tillotson and the school that followed him. He did not lay aside justification by faith, and the need of grace, for semi-heathen disquisitions about morality and duty, virtue and vice. And he was quite right. Laud and his followers went infinitely beyond the doctrines of our Church. Tillotson and his school fell infinitely below.

But if a churchman is a man who reads the Articles, and Liturgy, and Homilies, in the sense of the men who compiled them—if a churchman is a man who sympathizes with Cranmer, and Latimer, and Hooper, and

Jewell—if a churchman is a man who honors doctrines and ordinances in the order and proportion that the Thirty-nine Articles honor them—if this be the true definition of a churchman, then Whitefield was the highest style of churchman—as true a churchman as ever breathed. And as for Whitefield's adversaries, they were little better than shams and impostors. They had place and power on their side, but they scarcely deserve to be called churchmen at all.

Perhaps no better test of Whitefield's religious opinions can be supplied, than the list of authors in divinity which he wrote out for the use of a college connected with his orphan house in Georgia. Of churchmen, this list includes the names of Archbishop Leighton, Bishop Hall, and Burkitt; of Puritans, Pool, Owen, and Bunyan; of Dissenters, Matthew Henry and Doddridge; of Scotch Presbyterians, Wilson and Boston. All these are men whose praise is even now in all the churches. These, let us understand, were the kind of men with whom he was of one mind in doctrine.

As to the substance of Whitefield's theological teaching, the simplest account I can give of it is, that it was purely Evangelical. There were four main things that he never lost sight of in his sermons. These four were:

1. Man's complete ruin by sin, and consequent natural corruption of heart,
2. Man's complete redemption by Christ, and complete justification before God by faith in Christ,
3. Man's need of regeneration by the Spirit, and entire renewal of heart and life, and
4. Man's utter want of any title to be considered a living Christian, unless he is dead to sin and lives a holy life.

Whitefield had no notion of flattering men, and speaking smooth things to them, merely because they were baptized and called Christians, and sometimes came to church. He only looked at one prominent feature in the thousands he saw around him; and that was, the general character of their lives. He saw the lives of these multitudes were utterly contradictory to the Bible, and utterly at variance with the principles of the church to which they professed to belong. He waited for nothing more. He looked for no further evidence. He judged of trees by their fruits. He told these thousands at once that they were in danger of being lost forever—that they were in the broad way that leads to destruction—that they were dead, and must be made alive again—that they were lost, and must be found. He told them that if they loved life, they must immediately repent—they must become new creatures—they must be converted, they must be born again. And I believe the apostles would have done just the same.

But Whitefield was just as full and explicit in setting forth the way to heaven as he was in setting forth the way to hell. When he saw that men's consciences were pricked and their fears aroused, he would open the treasure-house of gospel mercy, and spread forth before a congregation its unsearchable stores. He would unfold to them the amazing love of God the Father to a fallen world—that love from which he gave his only-begotten Son, and on account of which, while we were yet sinners, Christ died for us. He would show them the amazing love of God the Son in taking our nature on him, and suffering for us, the just for the unjust. He would tell them of Jesus able to save to the uttermost all that would come to God by him—Jesus and his everlasting righteousness, in which the vilest sinners might stand complete and perfect before the throne of God—Jesus and the blood of sprinkling, which could wash the blackest sins away—Jesus, the High Priest, waiting to receive all who would come to him, and not only mighty, but ready to save. And all this glorious salvation, he would tell men, was close to them. It was not far above them, like heaven. It was not deep beneath them, like hell. It was near at hand. It was within their reach. He would urge them at once to accept it. The man that felt his sins and desired deliverance had only to believe and be saved, to ask and receive, to wash and be clean. And was he not right to say so? I believe the apostles would have said much the same.

But while Whitefield addressed the careless and ungodly masses in this style, he never failed to urge on those who made a high profession of religion their responsibility, and to stir them up to walk worthy of their high calling. He never tolerated men who talked well about religion but lived inconsistent lives. Such men, no doubt, there were about him, but it is pretty certain they got no quarter from him. On the contrary, one of his biographers tells us that he was especially careful to impress on all the members of his congregation the absolute necessity of adorning the doctrine of God in all the relations of life. Masters and servants, rich people and poor, old and young, married and single, each and all were plainly exhorted to glorify God in their respective positions.

One day he would tell the young men of his congregation to beware of being like one he heard of, whose uncle described him as such a jumble of religion and business, that he was fit for neither. Another day he would hold up the example of a widow, remarkable for her confidence in God. Another day he would say to them, "God convert you more and more every hour of the day; God convert you from lying in bed in the morning; God convert you from lukewarmness; God convert you from conformity to the world!" Another day he would warn young men against leaving their religion behind them as they rose in the world. "Beware," he would say, "of being golden apprentices, silver journeymen, and copper masters." In short, there never was a greater mistake than to suppose there was anything Antinomian or licentious in Whitefield's teaching. It was discriminating, unquestionably. Sinners had their portion; but saints had their portion too. And what was this but walking in the very steps of the apostle Paul?

The crowning excellence of Whitefield's teaching was that he just spoke of men, things, and doctrines, in the way that the Bible speaks of them, and the place that the Bible assigns to them. God, Christ, and the Spirit—sin, justification, conversion, and sanctification—impenitent sinners the most miserable of people—believing saints the most privileged of people—the world a vain and empty thing—heaven the only rest for the soul—the devil a tremendous and ever-watchful foe—

holiness the only true happiness—hell a real and certain portion for the unconverted; these were the kind of subjects which filled Whitefield's mind, and formed the staple of his ministry. To say that he undervalued the sacraments would be simply false. His weekly communions at the tabernacle are an answer that speaks for itself. But he never put the first things in Christianity second, and the second first. He never put doctrine below sacraments, and sacraments above doctrine. And who shall dare to blame him for this? He only followed the proportion of the Bible.

It is only fair to add, that Whitefield exemplified in his practice the religion that he preached. He had faults, unquestionably. I have not come here to make him out a perfect being. He often erred in judgment. He was often hasty, both with his tongue and with his pen. He had no business to say that Archbishop Tillotson knew no more of religion than Mahomet. He was wrong to set down some people as the Lord's enemies, and others as the Lord's friends, so precipitately as he sometimes did. He was to blame for styling many of the clergy letter-learned Pharisees, because they could not receive the doctrine of the new birth. But still, after all this has been said, there can be no doubt that, in the main, he was a holy, self-denying, and consistent man. Even his worst enemies can say nothing to the contrary.

He was, to the very end, a man of eminent self-denial. His style of living was most simple. He refused money when it was pressed upon him, and once to the amount of £7000. He amassed no fortune. He founded no wealthy family. The little money he left behind him at his death was entirely from the legacies of friends.

He was a man of remarkable disinterestedness and singleness of eye. He seemed to live for only two objects—the glory of God, and the salvation of souls. He raised no party of followers who took his name. He established no system, like Wesley, of which his own writings should be cardinal elements. A frequent expression of his is most characteristic of the man: "Let the name of George Whitefield perish, so long as Christ only is exalted."

Last, but not least, he was a man of extraordinary liberality in his religion. He knew nothing of that narrow-minded policy which prompts a man to fancy that everything must be barren outside his own camp, and that his party has got a monopoly of truth and heaven. He loved all who loved the Lord Jesus Christ in sincerity. He measured all by the measure which the angels of God use—"did they possess repentance towards God, faith towards the Lord Jesus Christ, holiness of conversation?" If they did, they were as his brethren. His soul was with such men, by whatever name they were called. Minor differences were wood, hay, and stubble to him. The marks of the Lord Jesus were the only marks he cared for. This liberality is the more remarkable, when the spirit of the times he lived in is considered.

Even the Erskines, in Scotland, wanted him to preach for no other denomination but their own, viz., the Secession Church. He asked them, why only for them; and received the notable answer, that they were the Lord's people. This was more than Whitefield could stand. He asked if there were no other Lord's people but themselves. He told them, if all others were the devil's people, they certainly had more need to be preached to. And he wound up by informing them, that if the pope himself would lend him his pulpit, he would gladly proclaim the righteousness of Christ in it.

To this liberality of spirit he adhered all his days. And nothing could be a weightier testimony against all narrowness of spirit among believers, than his request shortly before his death, that when he did die, John Wesley might be asked to preach his funeral sermon. Wesley and he had long ceased to see eye to eye on Calvinistic points. But as Calvin said of Luther, so Whitefield was resolved to think of Wesley. He was determined to sink minor differences, and to know him only as a good servant of Jesus Christ.

Such was George Whitefield's religion. Comment, I hope, is needless upon it. Time, at any rate, forbids me to dwell on it a moment longer. But surely I think I have shown enough to justify me in expressing a wish that we had many living ministers in the Church of England like George Whitefield.

* * * * *

Historical Notes

George Whitefield deplored lukewarm Christianity. To him, it was worse than no faith at all. As a result, much of his ministry was focused on shaking churchgoers out of their lethargy. Whitefield often reminded his readers of the Laodocean message of Revelation 3:16, where Christ warned the church that He would spew such congregations out of his mouth. The only kind of faith that pleased God was fervent, heartfelt belief--a faith which Whitefield preached dramatically about.

Not everyone appreciated his methods. Because Whitefield often shouted and/or gestured, many pulpits in "respectable" churches soon closed to his preaching. When this happened, Whitefield took his messages outside, often preaching in meadows at the edges of cities==a practice that was considered nothing less than sacrilege to the "proper" church folks of his day.

Although some conservatives were still bothered by Whiiefield's style of preaching, the American colonies welcomed him when he arrived in the late 1730's. Together with several other zealous ministers (e.g. Jonathan Edwards, Gilbert Tennent, David Brainerd, and the Wesley brothers), George Whitefield rekindled believer's faith in Christ. The revival of the Great Awakening was an event in which all of the colonies shared, giving them a common, unifying experience which was seen by some as a preparation for the American Revolution which followed in the late 1700's.

Chapter 4: The Preaching of George Whitefield

The next part of the subject is one which I feel some difficulty in handling. I allude to Whitefield's preaching.

I find that this point is one on which much difference of opinion prevails. I find many are disposed to think that part of Whitefield's success is attributable to the novelty of gospel doctrines at the time when he preached, and part to the extraordinary gifts of voice and delivery with which he was endowed, and that the matter and style of his sermons were in no wise remarkable. From this opinion I am inclined to dissent altogether. After calm examination, I have come to the conclusion that Whitefield was one of the most powerful and extraordinary preachers the world has ever seen. My belief is, that hitherto he has never been too highly estimated, and that, on the contrary, he does not receive the credit he deserves.

One thing is abundantly clear and beyond dispute, and that is, that his sermons were wonderfully effective. No preacher has ever succeeded in arresting the attention of such enormous crowds of people as those he addressed continually in the neighborhood of London. No preacher has ever been so universally popular in every country he visited, England, Scotland and America, as he was. No preacher has ever retained his hold on his hearers so entirely as he did for thirty-four years. His popularity never waned. It was as great at the end of his days as it was at the beginning. This of itself is a great fact. To command the ear of people for thirty-four long years and be preaching incessantly the whole time is something that the novelty of the gospel alone will not account for. The theory that his preaching was popular, because new, to my mind is utterly unsatisfactory.

Another thing is no less indisputable about his preaching, and that is, that it produced a powerful effect on people in every rank of life. He won the suffrages of high as well as low, of rich as well as poor, of learned as well as unlearned. If his preaching had been popular with none but the uneducated masses, we might have thought it possible there was little in it except a striking delivery and a loud voice. But facts are, unfortunately, against this theory too; and, under the pressure of these facts, it will be found to break down.

It is a fact that numbers of the nobility and gentry of Whitefield's day were warm admirers of his preaching. The Marquis of Lothian, the Earl of Leven, the Earl of Buchan, Lord Rae, Lord Dartmouth, Lord James A. Gordon, might be named, among others, besides Lady Huntingdon and a host of ladies.

It is a fact that eminent statesmen, like Bolingbroke and Chesterfield, were frequently his delighted hearers. Even the artificial Chesterfield was known to warm under Whitefield's eloquence. Bolingbroke has placed on record his opinion, and said, "He is the most extraordinary man in our times. He has the most commanding eloquence I ever heard in any person."

It is a fact that cool-headed men, like Hume the historian, and Franklin the philosopher, spoke in no measured terms of his preaching powers. Franklin has written a long account of the effect his sermons produced at Philadelphia. Hume declared that it was worth going twenty miles to hear him.

Now these are facts—simple, historical, and well-authenticated facts. What shall we say to them? I say that these facts are quite enough to prove that Whitefield's effectiveness was not owing entirely to delivery and voice, as some men would have us believe. Bolingbroke and Chesterfield, and Hume and Franklin, were not such weak men as to allow their judgments to be biased by any mere external endowments. They were no mean judges of eloquence. They were, probably, among the best qualified critics of the day. And I say confidently, that their opinion can only be explained by the fact, that Whitefield was indeed a most powerful and extraordinary preacher.

But still, after all, the question remains to be answered, What was the secret of Whitefield's unparalleled success as a preacher? How are we to account for his sermons producing effects which no sermons, before or after his time, have ever yet done? These are questions you have a right to ask. But they are questions I find it very hard to answer. That his sermons were not mere voice and rant, I think we have pretty clearly proved. That he was a man of commanding intellect and grasp of mind, no one has ever pretended to say. How then are we to account for the effectiveness of his preaching?

The reader who turns for a solution of this question to the seventy-five sermons published under his name, will probably be much disappointed. He will not find in them many striking thoughts. He will not discover in them any new exhibitions of gospel doctrine. The plain truth is, that by far the greater part of them were taken down in short-hand by reporters, without Whitefield's knowledge, and published without correction. No intelligent reader, I think, can help discovering that these reporters were, most unhappily, ignorant alike of stopping and paragraphing, of grammar and of gospel. The consequence is, that many passages in these sermons are what Latimer would call a "mingle-mangle," or what we should call in this day "a complete mess."

Nevertheless, I am bold to say, that with all their faults, Whitefield's printed sermons will repay a candid perusal. Let the reader only remember what I have just said, that most of them are miserably reported, paragraphed and stopped, and make allowance accordingly. Let him remember also, that English for speaking and English for reading are two different languages; and that sermons which preach well, always read ill. Remember these two things, I say, and I do believe you will find very much to admire in some of Whitefield's sermons. For myself, I can only say, I believe I have learned much from them, and, however great a heresy against taste it may appear, I should be ungrateful if I did not praise them.

And now let me try to point out to you what seem to me to have been the characteristic features of Whitefield's sermons. I may be wrong, but they appear to me to present just such a combination of excellences as is most likely to make an effective preacher.

First and foremost, you must remember, Whitefield preached a singularly pure gospel. Few men ever gave their hearers so much wheat and so little chaff. He did not get into his pulpit to talk about his party, his cause, his interest, or his office. He was perpetually telling you about your sins, your heart, and Jesus Christ, in the way that the Bible speaks of them. "Oh! the righteousness of Jesus Christ!" he would frequently say: "I must be excused if I mention it in almost all my sermons." This, you may be sure, is the cornerstone of all preaching that God honors. It must be preeminently a manifestation of truth.

For another thing, Whitefield's preaching was singularly lucid and simple. You might not like his doctrine, perhaps; but at any rate you could not fail to understand what he meant. His style was easy, plain, and conversational. He seemed to abhor long and involved sentences. He always saw his mark and went direct at it. He seldom or never troubled his hearers with long arguments and intricate reasonings. Simple Bible statements, pertinent anecdotes, and apt illustrations, were the more common weapons that he used. The consequence was that his hearers always understood him. He never shot above their heads. Never did man seem to enter so thoroughly into the wisdom of Archbishop Usher's saying, "To make easy things seem hard is easy, but to make hard things easy is the office of a great preacher."

For another thing, Whitefield was a singularly bold and direct preacher. He never used that indefinite expression, "we," which seems so peculiar to English pulpit oratory, and which leaves a hearer's mind in a state of misty confusion as to the preacher's meaning. He met men face to face, like one who had a message from God to them—like an ambassador with tidings from heaven; "I have come here to speak to you about your soul." He never minced matters or beat about the bush in attacking prevailing sins. His great object seemed to be to discover the dangers his hearers were most liable to, and then fire right at their hearts. The result was that hundreds of his hearers used always to think that the sermons were specially addressed to themselves. He was not content, like many, with sticking on a tailpiece of application at the end of a long discourse. A constant vein of application run through all his sermons. "This is for you: this is for you: and this is for you." His hearers were never let alone. Nothing, however, was more striking than his direct appeals to all classes of his congregation, as he drew towards a conclusion. With all the fault of his printed sermons, the conclusions of some of them are, to my mind, the most stirring and heart-searching addresses to souls that are to be found in the English language.

Another striking feature in Whitefield's preaching was his thundering earnestness. One poor, uneducated man said of him that he "preached like a lion." Never, perhaps, did any preacher so thoroughly succeed in showing people that he, at least, believed all he was saying, and that his whole heart, and soul, and strength, were bent on making them believe it too. No man could say that his sermons were like the morning and evening gun at Portsmouth, a formal discharge, fired off as a matter of course, that disturbs no body. They were all life. They were all fire. There was no getting away from under them. Sleep was next to impossible. You must listen, whether you liked it or not. There was a holy violence about him. Your attention was taken by storm. You were fairly carried off your legs by his energy, before you had time to consider what you would do. An American gentleman once went to hear him, for the first time, in consequence of the report he heard of his preaching powers. The day was rainy, the congregation comparatively thin, and the beginning of the sermon rather heavy. Our American friend began to say to himself, "This man is no great wonder, after all." He looked around and saw the congregation as little interested as himself. One old man, in front of the pulpit, had fallen asleep. But all at once Whitefield stopped short. His countenance changed. And then he suddenly broke forth in an altered tone: "If I had come to speak to you in my own name, you might well rest your elbows on your knees, and your heads on your hands, and sleep; and once in a while look up and say, what is this babbler talking of? But I have not come to you in my own name. No! I have come to you in the name of the Lord of Hosts," (here he brought down his hand and foot with a force that made the building ring,) "and I must and will be heard." The congregation started. The old man woke up at once. "Ay, ay!" cried Whitefield, fixing his eyes on him, "I have waked you up, have I? I meant to do it. I am not come here to preach to sticks and stones: I have come to you in the name of the Lord God of Hosts, and I must and will have an audience." The hearers were stripped of their apathy at once. Every word of the sermon was attended to. And the American gentleman never forgot it.

Another striking feature in Whitefield's preaching was his singular power of description. The Arabians have a proverb which says, "He is the best orator who can turn men's ears into eyes." If ever there was a speaker who succeeded in doing this, it was Whitefield. He drew such vivid pictures of the things he was dwelling upon, that his hearers could believe they actually saw them all with their own eyes and heard them with their own ears.

On one occasion, says one of his biographers, Lord Chesterfield was among his hearers. The preacher, in describing the miserable condition of a poor, benighted sinner, illustrated the subject by describing a blind beggar. The night was dark; the road dangerous and full of snares. The poor sightless mendicant is deserted by his dog near the edge of a precipice and has nothing to grope his way with but his staff. But Whitefield so warmed with his subject, and unfolded it with such graphic power, that the whole auditory was kept in breathless silence over the movements of the poor old man; and, at length, when the beggar was about to take that fatal step which would have hurled him down the precipice to certain destruction, Lord Chesterfield actually made a rush forward to save him, exclaiming aloud, "He is gone! he is gone!" The noble lord had been so entirely carried away by the preacher, that he forgot the whole was a picture.

One more feature in Whitefield's preaching deserves special notice, and that is, the immense amount of pathos and feeling which it always contained. It was no uncommon thing with him to weep profusely in the pulpit. Cornelius Winter goes so far as to say that he hardly ever knew him get through a sermon without tears. There seems to have been nothing whatever of affectation in this. He felt intensely for the souls before him, and his feeling found a vent in tears. Of all the ingredients of his preaching, nothing, I suspect, was so powerful as this. It awakened sympathies, and touched secret springs in men, which no amount of intellect could have moved. It melted down the prejudices which many had conceived against him. They could not hate the man who wept so much over their souls. They were often so affected as to shed floods of tears themselves.

"I came to hear you," said one man, "intending to break your head; but your sermon got the better of me—it broke my heart." Once become satisfied that a man loves you, and you will listen gladly to anything he has got to say. And this was just one grand secret of Whitefield's success.

And now I will only ask you to add to this feeble sketch, that Whitefield's action was perfect—so perfect that Garrick, the famous actor, gave it unqualified praise—that his voice was as wonderful as his action—so powerful, that he could make thirty thousand people hear him at once; so musical and well-attuned, that men said he could raise tears by his pronunciation of the word "Mesopotamia:" that his fluency and command of extemporaneous language were of the highest order, prompting him always to use the right word and to put it in the right place. Add, I say, these gifts to those already mentioned, and then judge for yourselves whether there is not sufficient, and more than sufficient, in our hands, to account for his power as a preacher.

For my part, I say, unhesitatingly, that I believe no living preacher ever possessed such a combination of excellences as Whitefield. Some, no doubt, have surpassed him in some of his gifts; others, perhaps, have been his equals in others. But, for a combination of pure doctrine, simple and lucid style, boldness and directness, earnestness and fervor, descriptiveness and picture-drawing, pathos and feeling—united with a perfect voice, perfect delivery, and perfect command of words, Whitefield, I repeat, stands alone. No man, dead or alive, I believe, ever came alongside of him. And I believe you will always find, that just in proportion as preachers have approached that curious combination of excellences which Whitefield possessed, just in that very proportion have they attained what Clarendon defines true eloquence to be, e.g., "a strange power of making themselves believed."

* * * * *

Historical Notes

It would not be an exaggeration to describe George Whitefield as somewhat of a celebrity in his day. If preaching today, he would no doubt appear on the covers of People and Time magazines, or be interviewed on 60 Minutes and Good Morning, America. With his riveting style, Whitefield was the "Grand Itinerant," the traveling preacher with no home church who toured the colonies seven times from the 1730s to the 1760s, delivering open-air sermons that left his huge audiences spellbound, penitent, and "awakened" (thus the term "Great Awakening"). He also impressed Benjamin Franklin, who wrote the following fascinating passage about Whitefield in the pages of his diary:

In 1739 arriv'd among us from England the Rev. Mr. Whitefield, who had made himself remarkable there as an itinerant Preacher. He was at first permitted to preach in some of our Churches; but the Clergy taking a Dislike to him, soon refus'd him their Pulpits and he was oblig'd to preach in the Fields. The Multitudes of all Sects and Denominations that attended his Sermons were enormous and it was [a] matter of Speculation to me who was one of the Number, to observe the extraordinary Influence of his Oratory on his Hearers, and how much they admir'd and respected him, notwithstanding his common Abuse of them, by assuring them they were naturally half Beasts and half Devils. It was wonderful to see the Change soon made in the Manners [behavior] of our Inhabitants; from being thoughtless or indifferent about Religion, it seem'd as if all the World were growing Religious; so that one could not walk thro' the Town in an Evening without Hearing Psalms sung in different Families of every Street.

I happened soon after to attend one of his Sermons, in the Course of which I perceived he intended to finish with a Collection, and I silently resolved he should get nothing from me. I had in my Pocket a Handful of Copper Money, three or four silver Dollars, and five Pistoles [Spanish coins] in Gold. As he proceeded I began to soften, and concluded to give the Coppers. Another Stroke of his Oratory made me asham'd of that, and determin'd me to give the Silver; and he finish'd so admirably, that I emptied my Pocket wholly into the Collector's Dish, Gold and all. At this Sermon there was also one of our Club [Junto literary club], who being of my Sentiments respecting [opinions concerning] the Building in Georgia, and suspecting a Collection might be intended, had by Precaution emptied his Pockets before he came from home; towards the Conclusion of the Discourse [sermon], however, he felt a strong Desire to give, and apply'd to a Neighbor who stood near him to borrow some Money for the Purpose. The Application was unfortunately to perhaps the only Man in the Company [audience] who had the firmness not to be affected by the Preacher. His Answer was, At any other time, Friend Hopkinson, I would lend to thee freely; but not now; for thee seems to be out of thy right Senses.

Of George Whitefield's ability to speak to large crowds and be heard, Benjamin Franklin stated that:

He had a loud and clear Voice, and articulated his Words and Sentences so perfectly that he might be heard and understood at a great Distance, especially as his Auditors [audience], however numerous, observ'd the most exact Silence. He preach'd one Evening from the Top of the Court House Steps, which are in the middle of Market Street, and on the West Side of Second Street which crosses it at right angles. Both Streets were fill'd with his

Hearers to a considerable Distance. Being among the hindmost in Market Street, I had the Curiosity to learn how far he could be heard, by retiring backwards down the Street towards the River; and I found his Voice distinct till I came near Front Street, when some Noise in that Street, obscur'd it. Imagining then a Semicircle, of which my Distance should be the Radius, and that it were fill'd with Auditors, to each of whom I allow'd two square feet, I computed that he might well be heard by more than Thirty Thousand. This reconcil'd me to the Newspaper Accounts of his having preach'd to 25,000 People in the Fields, and to the ancient Histories of Generals haranguing whole Armies, of which I had sometimes doubted.

Chapter 5: The Work of George Whitefield

And now, there only remains one more point connected with Whitefield to which I wish to advert. I fear that I shall have exhausted your attention already. But the point is one of such importance, that it cannot be passed over in silence. The point I mean is, the actual amount of real good that Whitefield did.

You will, I hope, understand me, when I say, that the materials for forming an opinion on this point in a history like his, must necessarily be scanty. He founded no denomination among whom his name was embalmed, and his every act recorded, as did John Wesley. He headed no mighty movement against a church which openly professed false doctrines, as Luther did against Rome. He wrote no books which were to be the religious classics of the millions, like John Bunyan. He was a simple, guileless man who lived for one thing only, and that was to preach Christ. If he succeeded in doing that effectually, he cared for nothing else. He did nothing to preserve the memory of his usefulness. He left his work with the Lord.

Of course, there are many people who can see in Whitefield nothing but a fanatic and enthusiast, There is a generation that loathes everything like zeal in religion. There are never wanting men of a cautious, cold-blooded, Erasmus-like temper, who pass through the world doing no good, because they are so dreadfully afraid of doing harm. I do not expect such men to admire Whitefield, or allow he did any good. I fear, if they had lived eighteen hundred years ago, they would have had no sympathy with St. Paul.

Again, there are other people who count schism a far greater crime than either heresy or false doctrine. There is a generation of men who under no circumstances will worship God out of their own parish: and as to separation from the Church, they seem to think that nothing whatever can justify it. I do not, of course, expect such men to admire Whitefield or his work. His principle evidently was, that it was far better for men to be uncanonically saved than canonically damned.

Whether by any other line of action Whitefield could have remained in the church, and retained his usefulness, is a question which, at this distance of time, we are very incompetent to answer. That he erred in temper and judgment in his dealings with the bishops and clergy, in many instances, I have no doubt. That he raised up fresh bodies of separatists from the Church of England, and made breaches which probably will never be repaired, I have no doubt also. But still it must never be forgotten, that the state of the church was bad enough to provoke a holy indignation. The old principle is most true, that "he is the schismatic who causes the separation, and not he who separates." If Whitefield did harm, the harm ought to be laid on the church which compelled him to act as he did, quite as much as on him. And when we come to strike the balance, I believe the harm he may have done is outweighed by the good a thousandfold.

The truth, I believe, is, that the direct good Whitefield did to save souls was enormous. I will go farther. I believe it is incalculable. In Scotland, in England, in America, credible witnesses have recorded their testimony that he was the means of converting thousands of souls.

Franklin, the philosopher, was a cold, calculating man, and not likely to speak too highly of any minister's work. Yet even he confessed that it "was wonderful to see the change soon made by his preaching in the manners of the inhabitants of Philadelphia. From being thoughtless or indifferent about religion, it seemed as if all the world were growing religious."

Maclaurin and Willison were Scotch ministers, whose names are well-known to theological readers and stand deservedly high. Both of them have testified that Whitefield did an amazing work in Scotland. Willison, in particular, says: "That God honored him with surprising success among sinners of all ranks and persuasions."

Old Venn, in our own church, was a man of strong common sense, as well as great grace. His opinion was, that "if the greatness, extent, success, and disinterestedness of a man's labors can give him distinction among the children of Christ, then we are warranted to affirm, that scarce any one has equaled Mr. Whitefield." Again, he says, "It is a well-known fact that the conversion of men's souls has been the fruit of a single sermon from his lips, so eminently was he made a fisher of men." And again, "Though we are allowed to sorrow that we shall never see or hear him again, we must still rejoice that millions have heard him so long, so often, and to such good effect; and that out of this mass of people, multitudes are gone before him to hail his entrance into the world of glory."

John Newton was a shrewd man, as well as an eminent minister of the gospel. His testimony is, "I am not backward to say, that I have not read or heard of any person, since the apostles' days, of whom it may more emphatically he said, he was a burning and a shining light, than the late Mr. Whitefield, whether we consider the warmth of his zeal, the greatness of his ministerial talents, or the extensive usefulness with which the Lord honored him."

These are not solitary testimonies. I might add many more if time permitted. Romaine did not agree with him in many things, yet what does he say of him? "We have none left to succeed him; none, of his gifts; none, anything like him in usefulness." Toplady was a tremendously high Calvinist, and not disposed to overestimate the number of saved souls. Yet he says, Whitefield's ministry was "attended with spiritual benefit to tens of thousands;" and he styles him "the apostle of the British empire, and the prince of preachers." Hervey was a quiet, literary man, whose health seldom allowed him to quit the retirement of Weston Favell. But he says of Whitefield, "I never beheld so fair a copy of our Lord, such a living image of the Savior. I cannot forbear applying the wise man's encomiums of an illustrious woman to this eminent minister of the everlasting gospel: 'Many sons have done virtuously, but thou excellest them all.'"

But if the amount of direct good that Whitefield did in the world was great, who shall tell us the amount of good that he did indirectly? I believe it never can be reckoned up. I suspect it will never be fully known until the last day.

Whitefield was among the first who stirred up a zeal for the pure gospel among the clergy and laity of our own church. His constant assertion of pure Reformation principles—his repeated references to the Articles, *Prayer Book*, and Homilies—his never-answered challenges to his opponents to confute him out of the Formularies of their own communion—all this must have produced an effect and set many thinking. I have no doubt whatever, that many a faithful minister, who became a shining light in those days within the Church of England, first lighted his candle at the lamp of a man outside.

Whitefield, again, was among the first to show the right way to meet infidels and skeptics. He saw clearly that the most powerful weapon against such men is not metaphysical reasoning and critical disquisition; but preaching the whole gospel, living the whole gospel, and spreading the whole gospel. It was not the writings of Leland, and the younger Sherlock, and Waterland, and Leslie, that rolled back the flood of infidelity one half so much as the preaching of Whitefield, and Wesley, and Fletcher, and Romaine, and Berridge, and Venn. Had it not been for them, I firmly believe we might have had a counterpart of the French Revolution in our own land. They were the men who were the true champions of Christianity. Infidels are seldom shaken by mere abstract reasoning. The surest arguments against them are gospel truth and gospel life.

To crown all, Whitefield was the very first who seems thoroughly to have understood what Chalmers has called the aggressive system. He did not wait for souls to come to him, but he went after souls. He did not sit tamely by his fireside, mourning over the wickedness of the land. He went forth to beard the devil in his high places. He attacked sin and wickedness face-to-face and gave them no peace. He dived into holes and corners after sinners. He hunted up ignorance and vice wherever it could be found. He showed that he thoroughly realized the nature of the ministerial office. Like a fisherman, he did not wait for the fish to come to him. Like a fisherman, he used every kind of means to catch souls. Men know a little more of this now than they did formerly. City missions and district visiting societies are evidences of clearer views. But let us remember this was all comparatively new in Whitefield's time, and let us give him the credit he deserves.

In short, I come to the conclusion that no man has ever done more good in his day and generation than the man who is the subject of this lecture. He was a true hero, and that in its highest and best sense. He did a work that will stand the fire, and glorify God, when many other works are forgotten. And for that work I believe that England owes a debt to his character which England has never yet paid.

* * * * *

Historical Notes

Largely forgotten today, George Whitefield was probably the most famous religious figure of the eighteenth century. Newspapers called him the "marvel of the age." Whitefield was a preacher capable of commanding thousands on two continents through the sheer power of his oratory. In his lifetime, he preached at least 18,000 times to perhaps 10 million hearers. (Christianity Today)

Whitefield's oratory featured no ordinary sermons. He portrayed the lives of biblical characters with a realism no one had seen before. He cried, he danced, he screamed. Among the enthralled was David Garrick, then the most famous actor in Britain. "I would give a hundred guineas," he said, "if I could say 'Oh' like Mr. Whitefield."

Whitefield is remembered as one of the first to preach to slaves. In an age when crossing the Atlantic Ocean was a long and hazardous adventure, he visited America seven times, making 13 ocean crossings in total. It is estimated that throughout his life, he preached more than 18,000 formal sermons, of which 78 have been published. In addition to his work in North America and England, he made 15 journeys to Scotland, two journeys to Ireland, and one each to Bermuda, Gibraltar, and the Netherlands. In England and Wales, Whitefield's itinerary included every county.

He went to the Georgia Colony in 1738 following John Wesley's departure, to serve as a colonial chaplain at Savannah. While in Georgia, Whitefield served as minister for an orphanage and traveled extensively throughout both North America and Britain in an effort to raise money for the orphanage. He would often preach and attend public events during his travels, which served to further spread his message.

Conclusion

And now, I hasten to a conclusion. I have set before you, to the best of my ability, Whitefield's time, and life, and religion, and preaching, and actual work. I have not extenuated his faults, to the best of my knowledge. I have not exaggerated his good qualities, so far as I am aware. It only remains for me to point out to you two great practical lessons which the subject appears to me to teach.

Learn then, I beseech you, for one lesson, the amazing power that one single man possesses, when he is determined to work for God and has got truth on his side.

Here is a man who starts in life with everything, to all appearance, against him. He has neither family, nor place, nor money, nor high connections on his side. His views are flatly opposed to the customs and prejudices of his time. He stands in direct opposition to the stream of public taste, and the religion of the vast bulk of ministers around him. He is as much isolated and alone, to all appearance, as Martin Luther opposing the pope, as Athanasius resisting the Arians, as Paul on Mars' Hill. And yet this man stands his ground. He arrests public attention. He gathers crowds around him who receive his teaching. He is made a blessing to tens of thousands. He turns the world upside down. How striking these facts are!

Here is your encouragement, if you stand alone. You have no reason to be cast down and faint-hearted. You are not weak, though few, if God is with you. There is nothing too great to be done by a little company, if only they have Christ on their side. Away with the idea that numbers alone have power! Cast away the old vulgar error that majorities alone have strength. Get firm hold of the great truth that minorities always move the world.

Think of the little flock that our Lord left behind him, and the one hundred and twenty names in that upper chamber in Jerusalem, who went forth to assault the heathen world! Think of George Whitefield assailing boldly the ungodliness which deluged all around him, and winning victory after victory! Think of all this. Cast fear away. Lay out your talents heartily and confidently for God.

Here also is your example, if you desire to do good to souls. Whether you become ministers or missionaries or teachers, never forget you must fight with Whitefield's weapons if you wish to have any portion of Whitefield's success. Never forget what John Wesley said was Whitefield's theology—"Give God all the glory of whatever is good in man: set Christ as high and man as low as possible, in the business of salvation. All merit is in the blood of Christ, and all power is from the Spirit of Christ."

Think not for a moment that earnestness alone will insure success. This is a huge delusion. It will do nothing of the kind. All the earnestness in the world will never enable a teacher of German theology to show you one Tinnevelly, or a teacher of semi-popery one Sierra Leone. Oh, no! it must be the simple, pure, unadulterated gospel that you must carry with you, if you are to do good. You must sow as Whitefield sowed, or you will never reap as he reaped.

Learn, in the last place, what abundant reasons we have for thankfulness in the present condition of the Church of England.

We are far too apt to look at the gloomy side of things around us, and at that only. We are all prone to dwell on the faults of our condition, and to forget to bless God for our mercies. There are many things we could wish otherwise in our beloved church, beyond all question. There are defects we could wish to see remedied, and wounds we should gladly see healed. But still, let us look behind us, and compare the church of our day with the church of Whitefield's times. Look on this picture, and on that, and I am sure, if you do so honestly and fairly, you will agree with me that we have reason to be thankful.

We have bishops on the bench now, who love the simple truth as it is in Jesus, and are ready to help forward good works—bishops who are not ashamed to come forward in Exeter Hall, and lend their aid to the extension of Christ's gospel—bishops who would have welcomed a man like Whitefield, and found full occupation for his marvelous gifts. Let us thank God for this. It was not so a hundred years ago.

We have hundreds of clergymen in our parishes now, who preach as full a gospel as Whitefield did, though they may not do it with the same power—clergymen who are not ashamed of the doctrine of regeneration, and do not pronounce a minister a heretic, because he says to ungodly people, "Ye must be born again." Let us thank God for this. A man need not travel many miles now in order to find parishes where the gospel is preached. When driven out of one parish church, he can find truth in another. It was not so a hundred years ago.

We have thousands of laymen now who are fully alive to the duties and responsibilities of members of a Protestant church—laymen who rejoice in holding up the hands of Evangelical ministers, and are righteously jealous for the maintenance and extension of Evangelical truth. Let us thank God for this. It was not so a hundred years ago.

We have societies and agencies for evangelizing every dark corner of the earth in connection with our church. We have wide and effectual doors of usefulness for all who are willing to labor in the Lord's vineyard. The difficulty now is, not so much to find openings for doing good, as to find men. Let us thank God for this. It was not so a hundred years ago.

Young men of the Church of England, I ask you to gather up these facts, and treasure them in your memories. They are facts. They cannot be gainsaid. Treasure them up, I repeat. Look back a century, and then look around you, and then judge for yourselves whether you ought not to be thankful.

Beware, I beseech you, of that tribe of men who would fain persuade you to forsake the Church of England and separate from her communion. There is a generation of murmurers and complainers in the present day who seem to revel in picking holes—a generation that seems to forget that fault-finding is the easiest task in all the world—a generation that has no eyes to see the healthy parts in our body ecclesiastic, but has a wonderfully quick and morbid scent for detecting its sores—a generation that is mighty to scatter, but impotent to build—a generation that would persuade churchmen to strain at gnats, but finds no difficulty itself in swallowing camels—a generation that would have you pull the old house down, but cannot offer you so much as a tent in its place: of all such men, I say solemnly and affectionately—of all such men, I warn you to beware. Listen not to them. Have no friendship with them. Avoid them. Turn from them. Pass away.

Let us not leave the good old ship, the Church of England, until we have some better reason than can at present be seen. What though she be old and weather-beaten! What though, in some respects, she may want repair! What though some of the crew be not to be depended on! Still, with all her faults, the old ship is in far better trim than she was a century ago. Let us acknowledge her faults and hope they may yet be amended. But still, with all her faults, let us stick by the ship!

When the Thirty-nine Articles of the Church of England are repealed, and the *Prayer Book* and Homilies so altered as to be un-Protestantized—when regeneration and justification by faith are forbidden to be preached in her pulpits—when the queen, lords and commons, and laity, have assented to these changes—in short, when the gospel is driven out of the establishment—then, and not till then, it will be time for you and me to go out; but, till then, I say, *let us stick by the church!*

www.ingramcontent.com/pod-product-compliance
Lightning Source LLC
Chambersburg PA
CBHW060601100726
47907CB00005B/1474

* 9 7 8 1 6 1 1 0 4 7 0 5 9 *